a girlfriends gift

OTHER BOOKS BY
CARMEN RENEE BERRY AND
TAMARA TRAEDER

girlfriends: Invisible Bonds, Enduring Ties
(Wildcat Canyon Press, 1995)

The girlfriends Keepsake Book:
The Story of Our Friendship
(Wildcat Canyon Press, 1996)

girlfriends Talk About Men:
Sharing Secrets for a Great Relationship
(Wildcat Canyon Press, 1997)

girlfriends for life:
Friendships Worth Keeping Forever
(Wildcat Canyon Press, 1998)

a girlfriends gift

Reflections on the Extraordinary Bonds of Friendship

CARMEN RENEE BERRY
AND TAMARA TRAEDER

WILDCAT CANYON PRESS
A Division of Circulus Publishing Group, Inc.
Berkeley, California

a girlfriends gift: Reflections on the Extraordinary Bonds of Friendship

Copyright © 2000 by Carmen Renee Berry and Tamara C. Traeder

Editorial Director: Roy M. Carlisle
Copyeditor: Larissa Berry
Production Coordinator: Larissa Berry
Proofreader: Holly Taines White
Cover Photo: Archive Holdings/The Image Bank
Cover Design: Gordon Chun Design
Interior Design and Typesetting: Gordon Chun Design
Typographic Specifications: Body text set in Cochin; Heads set in Nuptual Script

Printed in Canada

Library of Congress Cataloging-in-Publication Data

Berry, Carmen Renee.
   A girlfriends gift: reflections on the extraordinary bonds of friendship/Carmen Renee Berry and Tamara Traeder.
      p. cm.
   ISBN 1-885171-43-9 (pbk. : alk. paper)
   1. Female friendship—Quotations, maxims, etc.
   2. Women—Psychology—Quotations, maxims, etc. I. Traeder, Tamara, 1960- II. Title.

BF575.F66 B447 2000
302.3′4′082—dc21   00-020073

Distributed to the trade by Publishers Group West
10 9 8 7 6 5 4 3 2 1

To Rene,
whose friendship is one of the most
precious gifts in my life.

—Carmen

To Linda,
a gifted writer and my truly faithful friend.

—Tamara

Contents

A Word from the Authors

Sometimes the best gifts come in the smallest packages. In the same way that a gentle hug from a girlfriend can communicate immense gratitude, or a simple card from your best friend can provide enough support to get through another challenging day, a single phrase can capture the loyalty and laughter, the strength and the solace we receive from those women we herald as our "girlfriends."

As we have gathered hundreds of stories from girlfriends all over the world, we've noticed that, from time to time, a brief statement can capture a mural of emotions—snippets that describe succinctly what being girlfriends is all about.

We knew exactly what Amy meant when she wrote to us about her girlfriend, "I have never laughed so loudly, cried so hard, talked so much, or been myself so easily as I have been with her." We shared Laura's joyful excitement over meeting her girlfriend soul mate when she wrote, "I knew we were a perfect match when I, an inveterate bug hater, watched her kill a bug on the ceiling by throwing a magazine at it." And Colleen captured how much we need our friends when she wrote to us, "My girlfriends have been there to get me a ladder when I'm hanging by a thread. They have saved me from myself on more than one occasion, and one day I'm going to figure out how to tell them how I feel about them." These short descriptions and observations speak volumes about the stamina, hilarity, and camaraderie we find in our bonds with other women.

So that you and your girlfriends can share and savor these wonderful quotes, we assembled this sampling, some of which you'll recognize from our past girlfriends books; others are newly mined from letters and e-mails we've received. The quotes that have no name following them are taken directly from our writings. Those with names (some actual, some changed to protect privacy) have been written by girlfriend contributors. Regardless of the source, we're sure you'll find just the right phrase to convey exactly what you feel in your heart about your girlfriends.

The Gift of
Friendship

Our Girlfriends' Gifts to Us

*O*ur modern society has never set much store by women's friendships, frequently dismissing them as shallow institutions, chiefly there to facilitate shopping expeditions and restroom visits. But the lucky women who have experienced the trust level and support that is available in female friendships know better.

We have proven that our love will weather the hardest storms and years of separation. Her friendship, in the face of all that has happened between us, is one of the most precious things in my life. —*Tracey*

Anyone who has shown that willingness to expose their darkest secrets or greatest fears to another woman understands the treasure of a trusted girlfriend.

Only someone with a special best friend would understand the closeness, love, fun, and most of all, the truth of a real friend. —*Kathy*

Jean has brought so much laughter into my life. She also would really listen to my problems, start thinking about solutions to them, and then would come back to me with suggestions—all without me asking her to do so. —*Lucy*

I truly believe you cannot be happy without your girlfriends. —*Cheri*

During our reunion, we decided that our continued relationship only confirmed what good choices we had all made as children. —*Pam*

Throughout my life, I have been blessed with the most wonderful friends. Some are forever friends, and some were friends of specific stages and seasons. —*Sandra*

Every once in a while Karen will send me a little note, and it will have a tea bag in it. The note will say, "I'm thinking of you. Have a cup of tea on me." I seem to receive these treasures from her whenever I need them most. —*Linda*

My girlfriends' love has helped me remember that I am lovable, even when the man in my life can't love me. I'll be forever grateful to them. —*Candi*

I owe a debt of gratitude to all the women friends I've ever had who taught me so much about trusting other women. By the time I met Sonya, I had so much trust in myself that I was able to fling myself into this relationship and trust her immediately. —*Vicky*

If our girlfriends can like us, we can like ourselves.

She is the type of friend that one person can only dream about having. —*Julia*

One companionable Saturday when we'd been reading silently for several hours, Karen looked up and commented, "You know, being with you is like being with myself." It was one of the highest compliments I have ever received. —*Suzy*

Our friendship has outlasted the relationships with men we thought we'd never get over. —*Sharon*

Karen and I are like twin stars, revolving around each other; young men weren't that significant — like less influential planets that circled our stellar attraction. —*Suzy*

I am forever indebted to Lisa, who knew me and believed in me more than I knew and believed in myself. —*Laurie*

Friendship is a gift that should be treasured and never taken for granted. I did it once, but never again. I have the world's best friend as my best friend and I am the luckiest person in the world for that. —*Elizabeth*

A good friend of mine typed my master's thesis for me. If she hadn't, I wouldn't have finished my degree—that has opened many doors for me.

—*Rachel Ann*

I often think, how could I have survived without these women? —*Claudette*

One of the things I most admire about my girlfriend is that I can say even the ugly stuff about myself to her. I'm realizing how important that is. I can say anything. —*KC*

I've always felt that I could say anything to Sue about my children, and she would always understand that it never diminished how much I loved them and adored them. We don't have to backtrack and add "And you know how much I really love this child." . . . There's no betrayal of the child in the discussion with each other, because the other mother, the one who's capable of being the good-enough mother in the moment, is there holding the good-enough part of the child. *—Bonnie*

If you are fortunate, you have a friend who is there when you need her, who can put matters into perspective or make you laugh, and who knows your worst mistakes and most unsavory fears about yourself and loves you anyway.

A true girlfriend appreciates our
support and is not offended by our bad moods
or scared by our tears.

A Sacred Relationship

Sometimes our girlfriends are the ones who become our spiritual families—people to whom, for whatever reason, we feel more comfortable going to with our confessions, problems, and achievements.

Authentic female friendship is when we allow another woman to see our core, go to our core, and risk sharing our souls. —*Sue*

I don't know what to say about Patty. She's my mentor, my friend, my spiritual guide. Her courage and wisdom inspire me. Her humility and faith awe me. Her grace and love encourage me. —*Tracey*

We have entrusted our deepest, darkest moments to each other. A deep friendship allows for dependence upon each other as well as support, courage, and honesty. —*Tanya*

She is my soul mate. —*Julia*

With our girlfriends, we peel back many layers of our personalities. This process is an intimate and, we believe, sacred undertaking.

I've never been much of a religious person, but I talked to God when times were tough. I truly believe that God's answer was Cyndi. I wouldn't be anywhere close to where I am now if Cyndi hadn't come into my life. I thank God every day for her. —*Lesli*

Many times we feel that our friends are sent to us from heaven. We do not often pause in our busy days to reflect on the "meant-to-be" quality of our relationships with other women.

My girlfriends have been there to get me a ladder when I'm hanging by a thread. They have saved me from myself on more than one occasion, and one day I'm going to figure out how to tell them how I feel about them. *—Colleen*

We come from and have arrived at many different religious and spiritual places, but before our weekends together end, we gather in a circle to talk, pray, voice personal concerns, and meditate— whatever feels right—with no pressure. It is such a positive gathering that we all leave eager, knowing we will meet again. *—Pam*

Somewhere in the past, the word "girlfriend" has become associated with the trivial, the inconsequential. We don't think so, and we officially, here and now, reclaim the word to describe our best, our crucial, friendships.

A true girlfriend prays for you
without being asked.

Like a Sister

*A*n interesting paradox arises when we describe our friends. Often wishing to illustrate the seriousness of the friendship or the closeness we feel toward a friend, we use the phrase "she's like my sister" or "my friends are my family." Yet many of us would not share the details of our inner lives and outer occupations with our families the way we do with our best girlfriends.

Even though I have two younger sisters, I can be more honest with my friends. My sisters and I share a painful childhood, and surviving it has brought us close, but there is too much history to easily feel like successful adults together. My friends mirror my growth.

—*Kathleen*

If we say that our friends are like our families, we mean we share the highest level of commitment to and acceptance of each other, even if our families do not, in reality, meet our needs or our expectations.

Shirley and I met seventeen years ago at a new teachers' workshop. She and I have been sister-friends ever since. —*Rhonda*

Our friends are able to help us through confusing or difficult situations with our families, or through the loneliness of losing a family member, or even not having a family at all.

My sisters and I live very different lives. I raise a family and work only part-time. Cynthia is a single mother and successfully manages an accounting career. Caroline is married, climbing the coporate career ladder, and probably will never have any children. If we were not sisters, we would probably not have a lot in common, as we each pursue different hobbies and interests. Yet our bond is unbreakable as we still have plenty to share, discuss, and argue about. *—Elizabeth*

Roles that we played in our families can reemerge with family members, resisting all efforts to change them. With friends, however, we can be seen as evolving, changing adults.

> I think there is a certain security and familiarity with one another that you usually just get with family. But we choose one another.
> —*Stephanie*

I went to visit my cousin in college and she introduced me, at the age of sixteen, to a friend of hers, Sam. Five years later, I tagged along with them to a local country and western dance bar. The next day, he invited us to his house to listen to records, and a year later, Sam and I were married. She was a bridesmaid in my wedding, and I was matron of honor in hers. We were even laboring together, although several states apart, as my third daughter and her first were born a mere eleven hours apart.

—*Elizabeth*

Whether we have sisters or not, we look for the archetype of the sister, the woman who knows us better than anyone, who shares everything with us, who loves us as a blood relation. These are our girlfriends.

A true girlfriend may be the first person
with whom we "feel at home."

The First Girlfriend

o relationship affects us more than our relationship with our mother. If that relationship has been painful, it may be several decades before a daughter can trust other women or appreciate women friends. If that primary relationship with our mother is positive, however, we learn how to be good women and good friends at the same time. Or are these the same thing?

My daughter came in one day and said, "Mother, I have decided who I want in the wedding and who my matron of honor is going to be." I said, "That's great. Who are the girls?" So she named off the bridesmaids, and then she looked at me and said, "I would like you to be my matron of honor." Well, the chills came and then the tears rolled down my face. I look back on that time, and I realize that that was the defining moment when I became not only her mother, but her best friend. —*Sally*

Of all the friendships with women that I have, the one I most cherish, that is most regular, most sustaining, and most satisfying is the friendship with my mother. I can't articulate the facets of our friendship, but they are deep, abiding, spiritual, intellectual, and long-standing. My mother is one of nine children, eight of whom were girls. She lived most of her youth surrounded by women, both in all-girl's boarding and day schools, and with her many sisters. She grew up in a time when children were to be seen and not heard, which pushed her and her sisters into a secret society of sorts. To this day she and her sisters, ages ranging from sixty-five to eighty, still talk and correspond an amazing amount. —*Betsy*

Perhaps I should consider myself different from most of the gals of my generation, because my first true girlfriend is my mom! My mom has been my mentor and greatest support system, especially during my thirty years of illness. —*Gloria*

My need for close friendships comes from my mother. By her example, she taught me to make and keep friends. At the age of eighty, she still has friends that she met decades ago. —*Sandra*

I must pay tribute to the women who taught me that "to have a friend is to be a friend," my mother and grandmother. There are not words to express the love and gratitude I feel for being a part of their legacy of friendship. It has created more joy in my life than they will ever know. They taught me how to look at people with my heart and not my eyes. Because of that gift, I have cried many tears of sorrow as well as joy, but I would not trade one of those tears for a life less troubled by the tears of my friends. —*Tracey*

A true girlfriend understands the power
of the mother-daughter relationship to mold,
comfort, irritate, support, or devastate one.

In the
Beginning

Childhood Treasures

hildhood friendships provided us with a stable foundation upon which we have built our own integrity and our ability to say to another woman, "You can count on me."

It all began at the community pool when Christine and I were just babies and our mothers met and began chatting. I was in need of a hat for my bald head and was given Christine's. We still have the hat and plan to pass it back and forth for our own children to wear. —*Tanya*

Lisa and I met when we were three years old. It was my first interaction with the outside world, and Lisa was the first person I remember that was my size. —*Nancy*

> Who knew that that first "hello" would span through thirty-eight years. —*Brenda*

It was the first day of sixth-grade health class. We were all lined up against the back wall of the classroom as the teacher gave us the dreaded seat assignments. We had never met before that day, but as we found out later, we were both praying not to be seated next to "that girl." Of course, we were. We managed to ignore each other for the entire quarter. God being more stubborn than we were, we ended up in the same homeroom the next year. —*Tracey*

Childhood friends are the ones we make because of proximity—living next door, attending the same churches, being roommates at camp. If those last a lifetime, it's because by some miracle we were able to find someone to mirror who we wanted to become or who we really are. —*Irene*

One day I turned around and said to her, "Do you have a pen I can borrow?" Throughout the day I used that pen until I loaned it to another friend, who in turn never gave it back to me. The next day in class she asked me, "Can I have my pen back?" I tried to avoid her and made up lame excuses as to why I wouldn't, or more like, couldn't, give it back. Finally after three days of this she let it go and we started talking. I am so glad I borrowed, well, more like took, a pen from her in seventh grade. —*Julia*

What set Karen apart when we met at age eleven was her boldness and her sense of humor. I thought she was the funniest person alive. —*Wynn*

There was something about this girl sitting next to me that caught my attention. Right then I knew she and I would be close friends, and I was right. —*April*

My cousin Ann Frances was my salvation in high school because I had no particularly close girl-friends where I lived. In our brief and infrequent visits, A.F. and I lamented the stupidity of teenage boys and how best to stop zits before they started. She was my hope that there were girls "like me" somewhere. There were, and I later found them, but in the meantime, she was an important teenage friend who held the same values, goals, and priorities. *—Elizabeth*

The sign of a true friendship is when you can not communicate for ages and you can go right back to where you were. *—Rose*

What I First Remember

I *t doesn't seem to matter to the life of the friend-ship whether that first fateful connection was a positive or negative one—so long as it was memorable.*

When Georgia and I met at the copy machine, I saw her as a stereotypical "East Coast preppie" and she pegged me as your "typical Californian." —*Laurie*

She did everything first. When she got her period first, she trained me in great detail on how to look pale, double over with cramps, and stagger to the nurse's office to be excused from classes, where we would lay on cots and talk and laugh until we were half sick. When I finally did begin to menstruate, the nurse sent a note home saying I was either very irregular or having two periods a month. I never could remember whose period I was having, hers or mine. —*Patricia*

Sometimes a shared and traumatic transition can turn strangers into close friends. The empathy created by sharing emotional experiences can be like a fast-drying glue to a new friendship. Whether a friend shares our feeling or merely understands it, her ability to make room for our emotion is invaluable. Especially when we share our tears, the comfort offered in those moments of vulnerability, the swollen-eyes, red-nosed openness, can mark the beginning of loving friendship.

Just as a pearl is formed from an irritating piece of sand in an oyster, precious friendships may develop after an annoying beginning.

She was everything I wanted to be—graceful, elegant, poised, and still open and warm.
—*Patrice*

We may feel the pull of a true friend right away, or the tie may be uncovered years later in some unexpected way. When we discover her is irrelevant. What matters is that she has become one of our nearest and dearest, and we cherish her friendship no matter when it deepens.

After her warm and gracious welcome, I realized Jinny didn't know any "strangers." —*Helen*

She stood out among the crowd for a few reasons. Standing nearly six feet tall, she towered over the others. But there was something very big about Laurie that had nothing to do with her physical stature. She was not someone to be ignored. To go unnoticed. —*Judy*

I knew the potential was there because of the way she looked at me while we talked. She had a penetrating, intimate stare—not one that was intimidating, but rather one that expressed genuine interest. —*Jill*

There was something special about the look in her eyes, and I thought she looked like someone I wanted to get to know. —*Nina*

Twice I've had a strong feeling that someone would be a close friend before I actually met her or spoke with her in person. Both times that person became a very close friend. —*Carolyn*

I met Judy at the children's park. I had a nine-month-old daughter and was seven months pregnant with another. She also had two very small children with her. I probably noticed her because she is the kind of natural pretty that turns heads—both male and female. She looked about my age, and looked as tired as I felt. It's a small town, and I had already heard through the rumor mill that a new doctor and his young family had recently moved to town. Feeling a hunch that she might be the "doctor's wife," I introduced myself, and a friendship was born. That was fourteen years ago, and she will always be my kindred spirit. *—Elizabeth*

Here she was in a very comfortable situation — she had grown up with this group of people — and I, being new, was in an uncomfortable one. Lisa made room for me, a new person, in her life and let me be myself. *—Nancy*

Susan's spontaneous and infectious laugh caused my stomach to cramp as my tears of laughter dribbled to the floor. I decided that day that I wanted to be like Susan or at least share a friendship. *—Mary*

They are out there waiting, all kinds of wonderful women who may be the next stars in our universe of friends. All we need is the faith that they will show themselves when we are ready for them. Haven't they always?

A true friend may have been made in one day — but we hold her close to our hearts every day thereafter.

Woman to Woman

We're Just Different than Men

Men are not women and so relating to men is, by definition, a different experience. Whether the cause is genetic or environmental, men and women experience life differently. One group has experienced centuries of overt power while the other is just trying to get the hang of it; one group frets about the size of their penises and the other about the size of their breasts; one group is rewarded for sexual conquests while the other worries about pregnancy; one group shaves their faces and the other shaves their legs. No matter how sensitive a man may be, he is not a woman and, by definition, he lives life from a different perspective than that of a woman.

Many women say that their women friends respond to their problems differently than do most of the men in their lives. While men tend toward a fix-it approach, women often simply provide a listening, sympathetic ear.

Men just aren't like women. They see things and solve problems in different ways. Men don't like to talk about their feelings, and women thrive on it. *—Julie*

Women keep their friendships over a lifetime while men may consider their co-workers from their last job to be their best friends. *—Kathy*

Women are so busy being all things to all people, especially their families, that few men, children, and co-workers are aware of their needs. But, unlike most males I have come into contact with, close female friends notice everything. *—Elizabeth*

When we look to men as reference points we lose sight of who we are as women. It is like trying to define an apple by comparing it to an orange. The apple, described in terms of the orange, will never have its own identity, appeal, and value; it will simply be "not an orange."

Often we do not have an accurate picture of ourselves, and it is a true girlfriend who helps us see ourselves more clearly.

A Fine Balance

*E*ver try to put two like-charged sides of magnets together? They push against each other. But turn one around, and smack! The two magnets snap together with a powerful pull. Girlfriends can be like magnets, drawn to each other not by similarities but by differences.

> We say that if the two of us were combined into one person we'd be perfect because of our very different skills. —*Marilyn*

I knew we were a perfect match when I, an inveterate bug hater, watched her kill a bug on the ceiling by throwing a magazine at it. —*Laura*

We've both had some ups and downs in our lives (some worse than others), but it seems like when one of us is down, the other is there to pick the other up. I think that is important in any solid relationship. *—Debbie*

Our healthy friendships have room in them for one of us to be more needy at times than the other, and for one of us to set boundaries for ourselves. Friendships can break off if both parties are not willing to recognize boundaries or eventually engage in a balanced give and take.

I can't tell you who I am without telling you who my girlfriend is. Our relationships with other women are part of the ground of our being. *—Sue*

All healthy friendships operate within boundaries mutually agreed upon by both parties.

I had a roommate who had a major calculus test and became temporarily dysfunctional (way before that word was popular). That is to say, the pressure to excel, to make the grades, to get into law school became so overwhelming that she basically freaked out and couldn't relax. We weren't particularly given to massive amounts of alcohol at that time, but there remained, for those intense college moments that popped up now and then, a bottle of J & B in the closet. I looked at my poor roommate, walked to the closet, pulled out the fifth of scotch, and poured a shot and forced her to drink it. It really did have an immediate therapeutic effect. She continued studying, went to bed, and, if I'm not mistaken, aced the test. Girlfriends can be indispensable (and a lot cheaper than therapists). *—Betsy*

A girlfriend who values her friendships will make the effort to drag herself out of her own absorbing problems to hear about, and help with, her girlfriend's struggles. It is sometimes hard to know who is helping whom, as girlfriends take turns listening, talking, and coming to the aid of each other.

The friendships we value most are those that have a natural rhythm of give and take and shared vulnerability that is mutually beneficial to both women involved.

I know she is my best friend because we
have lost track of how much we owe each other
and we truly don't care. *—Ellen*

She Provides a Safe Harbor

Surviving difficult family situations can be tough if not impossible to do alone. Often we can look back and point to one or two friends who offered us an escape or a point of sanity along the way.

> As I look back now, I realize I relied heavily on my friendship with Marla to bring order and sanity into my life. Today, because of our history together, a phone call or a simple nod from my friend can put things in perspective.
> —Dierdre

Without necessarily intending to do so, we continually help each other get through yet another change-filled day.

She always has time, insight, and understanding enough for ten. —Marilyn

> What may start as perhaps a simple conversation over tea—"If something happened to me, would you take care of my children?"—can become a life-changing promise.

I thought it would be a sin not to tell you about four women whom I have the privilege to call my friends. Two of these women, Christi and Jill, I have known for about ten years now. I kind of see them as a bridge to my angst-ridden teenage life. The other two, Nickie and Beth, are friends that I have made pretty recently. I see them as well as a bridge to my angst-ridden teenage life. —*Colleen*

Because confidentiality is a fundamental component of women's friendships, the girlfriend bond has, in many cases, taken on near sacred status as a safe place to confess misdeeds, admit failures, explore remedies, and, purely and simply, tell the truth.

Our shared humor not only makes us feel part of a select group where nothing has to be explained, but also provides a safe place to heal in times of trouble.

Most women expect trustworthiness in their girl-friends before true closeness can be achieved, but other women have to learn that vulnerability, their vulnerability, is required in order for them to achieve closeness with other women.

A true girlfriend is the person with whom you can sit comfortably in silence, and yet be the same individual to whom you have so much to say.

A Loving Heart Listens

*W*e sometimes show our support by simply being present with our friends. No advice is needed; no wisdom required. All we request is an understanding heart and a listening ear.

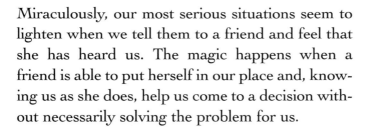

Miraculously, our most serious situations seem to lighten when we tell them to a friend and feel that she has heard us. The magic happens when a friend is able to put herself in our place and, knowing us as she does, help us come to a decision without necessarily solving the problem for us.

I wrote to Karen during those two A.M. hours of insomnia when marital or work anxiety beset me. Sometimes I wouldn't even mail them, although I started each letter "Dear Karen," with her eyes and ears as the intended audience. Somehow, just thinking she might read what I was thinking calmed me. After I'd poured my feelings on paper, I'd feel able to return to bed. *—Suzy*

My son was born very ill, with a congenital heart defect. It was the worst year of my life. My husband and I struggled with the fact we would probably lose our precious little boy. There were so many times that year that Dot knew exactly what was needed. The day I came home from the hospital without my son, she met me at my house with a table-cloth, cloth napkins, and turnovers. While our daughters played we sat over coffee and we were complete. I could talk or not talk, either was accepted. —*Diana*

Our sensitivity to one another's health or state of mind often stems from undiluted listening and paying attention, our antennae dialed in at a very delicate setting.

Plain and simple, she is a true friend who doesn't try to fix my problems, but lends her hand and her heart unselfishly. —*Amy*

My husband and I had been married for twenty-nine years and were in real trouble. Jenny was so loyal in her efforts to just be with me and let me express whatever I was feeling. I especially remember a time with her when I was feeling devastated; it seemed that my heart was literally breaking, and I laid my head in her lap and wept. She just let me do that, sitting with me, not judging me, not being angry at my husband, just giving me the permission to feel whatever I felt. That moment is so vivid— I remember where we were, how our bodies were situated, how my sobbing sounded. It was an intense, deep experience for me. —*Natasha*

She knows when to talk and when to listen and when to bring ice cream. —*Julia*

High-quality listening, even more so than high-quality advice, can keep us grounded and help us listen to our own hearts, finding our answers within ourselves.

Clarity and perspective are what we gain from our friends who hear us, really hear us, and take the time to stop other tasks and focus on what we are saying.

A true girlfriend doesn't offer what we consider "advice," but instead tends to be empathetic, eager to listen and reflect back to us what they are hearing.

We Always Have Fun
(Even Against the Odds)

Girlfriends worth keeping forever enrich our lives with humor and mischief, regardless of how "old" we become. We seem to revert back to giggles and allow ourselves unladylike guffaws over matters that only those in the friendship circle seem to appreciate.

Nickie is my portal to the absurd. When we get together, we laugh until we cry or cry until we laugh—it's pretty much all the same.

—Colleen

Nothing can bond you with your friend like escaping a scary-looking man who seems to be following you both, or the hilarity of watching American men gawk at topless women on a French beach.

Girlfriends often find themselves to be absolutely hilarious in each other's presence, while everyone else around them in those situations just rolls their eyes or stares in disbelief.

Girlfriends for life help each other find the courage to get through everything from rough days to life-changing decisions. Our shared laughter and fun put matters into perspective, even in the bleakest moments, and we encourage each other to take the steps in life that are right for us.

In the name of fun, girlfriends do a lot of healing. We laugh, we make plans, we take revenge, and, as a result, we help each other recover from everything from bad moods to bad relationships.

We have been accused of being drunk or crazy and, often, both. But we are merely laughing. The kind of laughter that sends your head back, makes your jaws ache, and runs tears down your cheeks. Those tears we have shared for many years and for many reasons. *—Judy*

Regardless of culture or time or distance, women bond together through laughter, dares, and crazy plans.

We wear nearly the same size in clothes, exact size in shoes, and have similar taste in fashions. I now live in Las Vegas and she still resides in Houston. Our big thrill when getting together twice a year is "trading." The traveling person packs for the trip including items that might make for good bartering. We go through the other's closet or luggage and swap. *—Rhonda*

Some of the enormously funny things we do with our girlfriends may seem unbelievably silly to everyone else. Asked why we did what we did, we can say only, "It seemed like a good idea at the time."

I took a trip with my high school best friend, and unfortunately, she was nauseated through the whole trip. I have pictures of her throwing up at all the landmarks in Paris, and when we got back, I put all of these pictures into a binder for her and titled it "Kathy's Movable Feast." —*Peg*

If there's a good line we both go for it. It's understood, and important, that you go for the good line. The grief and the joy are always all mixed up together. For me that's what makes the friendship so solid. —*Sue*

Sometimes it almost feels like twin language in that I will just say something and she knows exactly what I'm talking about, and she just screeches and thinks I'm hilarious. And it probably wasn't a bit funny to anyone else. —*Sue*

My friend and I wouldn't think of seeing a Mel Gibson movie without each other. It's practically a religious experience as we worship at The Altar of Mel.

Eileen and I have shared so much together— we've been poor together, been devastated by our divorces together, and survived and healed together. Her old car, "Luke the Buick," proved to be as unreliable as my old 1966 VW Beetle that sometimes got us where we were going, sometimes not. Most of the time, we didn't have much money to go anywhere anyway, so we just spent time together at each other's kitchen tables, sharing a cheap bottle of wine. —*Sandra*

Whether we're playing soccer as little girls, going to dances together as teenagers, or going on shopping sprees as adults, underneath the surface activity a deep bond is being forged. The actual activity is quite secondary, as women use these moments to share personal feelings, private longings, and their true essence with each other.

Christi is the clown. She can make me laugh at myself even when I'm crying. When I'm pissy and hating the world, Christi takes up my banner and hates with me until our haters are sore and then we laugh. *—Colleen*

I can call Sue and I can just be in a rage, and pretty soon I'm laughing. Or she's laughing at me. And that's the fabulous part of our friendship. *—Bonnie*

Give humor the honor it deserves. If we can keep each other laughing, we can keep each other sane.

Many times we have been at a movie or watching a television show, and something that is not supposed to be humorous sends us rolling down the aisles. I have felt very alone without her, chortling at something and finding people staring. Together we are the essence of silliness. This part of our friendship has saved us both from scary or sad situations.

—Vanessa

Sometimes life just seems too ridiculous and unexplainable. Laughing by yourself in these times seems somehow bitter and mirthless, but laughter shared with a friend feels sweet and healing.

When times are really grim, our friends' humor may save us from despair, even when the laughter might arise out of what seems to be a tragedy at the time.

It was the summer of 1972 and my friend Nancy and I were both fifteen years old. I had been invited to Mexico by her parents to spend a weekend outside of Ensenada on the beach. While touring in town, Nancy and I gained permission to go our own way provided we met her folks at a certain place by nightfall. Time got away from us, night came, and we lost our bearings. We decided which way we thought we should go and headed off. Soon we were in a neighborhood of questionable repute. I don't remember who initiated the idea, but in order to avoid the cat-calls from men and stop them from following us, we pretended to be more than just friends. Placing our arms around each other, we looked into each other's eyes while walking at breakneck speed for our destination. I'm not sure if at the end we were laughing at their disappointment or our own relief for having "gotten away." We were scolded by her parents for being late, but we didn't mind a bit. —*Heidi*

Despite the somber thread that binds us together, whenever I think of our relationship, I think of laughter. We each bring out the childish, playful, and sometimes sinister side of one another. This is evident every time we rag on someone and laugh the "wicked laugh," as we call it. *—Judy*

Laughter is the evidence of the fun we are having in the moment, but can also be a sign of healing and keeping our balance as life throws us curve balls. A hearty belly laugh, one that brings tears to our eyes and leaves us gasping, can make a lot of evils disappear.

A true girlfriend laughs at our jokes, especially the ones no one else thinks are funny.

Girlfriend Staying Power

We Hang in There
with Each Other

ince none of us know where the next turn of events will take us, looking to the future, with its uncertainties, can be a frightening prospect. However, our fears can be soothed by the certainty of friendship.

Beginning in junior high and continuing through high school graduation, Karen and I rode our bicycles to school together every single school day. I believe this was my first experience with commitment. We have delighted in each other's successes, laughed about the human condition, taken each other's side against real and imagined enemies, and coached one another through demanding times. When she asks, "What can I do for you?" I know I can give her an honest answer and that she'll deliver on her promise. *—Wynn*

My girlfriend is a real show-upper. If I have a party, and she might not feel well, she always comes for a little while. It's amazing to have a friend who really shows up, on whom you can rely. —*Elise*

Cathy's father died suddenly and I lost a very significant romantic relationship. We were both shell-shocked by our losses. Even though we weren't much company, we met together every week. Just having Cathy show up week after week meant so much. About a year later, when we were in a bit better shape, Cathy looked over at me and said, "Hey, I remember you." We laughed, and I realized that I didn't have to be in good shape to be loved by her. —*Carmen*

Does that mean I never let her down? Does that mean the rhythm is always in step? It means that in spite of, or including these issues, I absolutely can count on her. And what is so valuable is that I don't believe that is open to question. —*Catherine*

Like an enduring marriage, the bond between women friends survives life's struggles through sturdy commitment. That commitment has important consequences for each of the friends, a knowledge that someone is always on your side, a constancy on which you can call at any time.

She has always supported me in my decisions and is always there for me whenever I need her. —*Julia*

Who, at any age, doesn't find themselves getting annoyed by something we realize is essentially petty? Who doesn't deal with difficult feelings in a relationship? The sooner we learn from our mistakes with our friends, and develop the ability to apologize and the capacity to forgive, the longer our friendships last.

Many women have found that their girlfriends are there when no one else is; the level of commitment remains constant no matter what else is going on in their lives.

A true girlfriend makes room for you to mature, change, explore, and experiment. We make room for friendship that can stand the tests of time.

We Understand Each Other

Many women told us that as their friendships grew closer, one or both friends would start "knowing" things about the other without being told. From understanding each other so well that they finished each other's sentences to actually knowing that a friend was in trouble with no other indication that that was so, many women said their intuition was sharpened with a close friend.

> She knows my heart and my mind, and how I react to certain situations. And I know the same about her. —*Holly*

Deep friendships often result in knowing, frequently without asking, what the other feels and needs. Somehow our psyches become entwined, and we know things about each other that we have no rational reason to know—no one told us; it's not written down anywhere. Of course, we may not always know all of the whys and wherefores, but we get the sense that something is wrong, and we find out the details.

Friends can help. Just when you think your child is warped or something's going wrong or that you're a lousy parent, you talk about it in the group and somebody else laughs and says, "Oh, I went through that," or, "My child went through that." It affirms the fact that parenthood is a roller-coaster ride. It helps to know that we all face high and low points and that not one of us has a perfect child. —*Cheryl*

A lot has been written, seriously and facetiously, about women's need for communication and talking. Yet, with a really good friend, frequently no words are necessary.

Though our communication wanes at times of absence, I'm aware of a strength that emanates in the background. *—Claudette*

She understands me so well that she knows she periodically needs to drag me to the department store, lock me in the dressing room, and force me to try on new bras and panties. *—Alicia*

She always does her best to understand and does not judge me. *—Julia*

I have never laughed so loudly, cried so hard, talked so much, or been myself so easily as I have been with her. *—Amy*

Five friends and I gather each year to blow off steam, and among other things, crown with a tiara the woman who has the best (or worst) story about her family. It's the one time of the year we can be ourselves—not somebody's mom or wife. *—Ellen*

Understanding what our friends need isn't magic. It comes from our taking the time to notice one another and respond to the needs we see or sometimes only intuit.

Relaxed, secure, knowing the other understands our silences—these are the friendships that make us feel accepted, with no expectation to perform or be obligated to each other. Picking up where we left off is fine, and when we do so, we feel thoroughly nourished.

We share a bond with one another that is so strong that many times one of us has picked up the phone and called the other, only to hear her say, "I was just going to call you!" —*Melissa*

To this day, we finish each other's sentences, come up with really bizarre thoughts at the same time, and beat everybody at Pictionary. What would I do without her? —*Tracey*

She reappeared in my life when I really needed someone like her. She understands things that others might not because she and I are at the same point in our lives and share common goals. Plus, since we grew up together, she brings back a feeling of familiarity and we always treasure things from our past. —*Linda*

Girlfriends for life show they care for each other in myriad ways, with action that transcends mere affection. Lifelong friends pay attention, knowing, sometimes uncannily, when the other needs help, and then stepping in when necessary to do what is needed.

There are times when we could literally be each other. We go shopping a lot together, and I can pinpoint what she'll buy before she even tries it on. She knows my favorites, and I hers. She simply understands me, and I her. —*Aimee*

She knows what I am thinking even when I can't put it into words. —*Julia*

You know your friendship has withstood the test of time if you can pick up your conversation right where you left off, no matter how long it has been.

True girlfriends are those women who know you better than anyone (sometimes better than you know yourself).

My Staunch Defender

A friend will defend you when you can't defend yourself and stand up to tell the truth (or a lie, if necessary) to protect you.

> I thought I was being funny by putting myself down. I remember my friend Judy pulling me aside one time and saying, "You know, it's not funny anymore." Hearing that from her made me lighten up on constantly using myself as a butt of jokes. —*Katherine*

Sometimes our friends stand up for us by standing up to us. If they see us making choices or taking action that they feel will eventually hurt us, they try to stop us from following a self-damaging pattern that we cannot discern ourselves.

My girlfriend's ex-boyfriend refused to return her blender, and she was in no shape to see him again. I called and left message after message on his machine, but he refused to respond. Finally, I left a message saying, "I'm coming to your office tomorrow to make a scene." The blender mysteriously showed up on my girlfriend's porch that night. Sometimes we need someone to put their foot down and set things right. —*Pamela*

Loyalty can take the form of urging us to ask for what we want or need. Our girlfriends may show loyalty by rooting us on as we stand up for ourselves.

Jill is my strength, my backbone. She knows when to tell me I'm being silly and need to get over myself. And she knows when I really am in trouble; when I'm hurting and I won't let it out, she will pull it out of me and let me cry and howl until it's all good again. —*Colleen*

My girlfriends were incredibly loyal to the person I was and the person they knew I wanted to be.

—Tamara

There are times when we know we can count on our friends to draw from their fierce "mother bear" energy and stand up on our behalf.

One night I received an obscene phone call, with the threat that someone would soon come to my home. I called a friend who told me to stay on the line and pretend to be talking. I would know it was her when she rang the bell three times. She was there within ten minutes with her umbrella, and together we dealt with the unwanted caller.

—Genevieve

We may show loyalty to our friends by speaking up or merely showing up.

Our lives would be extremely difficult if we had to fight all of our battles alone. Knowing that someone is "on our side," the feeling that we have the reinforcing support that we need, can prevent our being overwhelmed when trouble comes.

Sometimes love is soft and sweet, nice and nurturing. But often the love that is needed is strong, confrontive, and clear. Sentimentality is tossed aside for the penetrating vision of someone who knows us well and cares enough to take us on. When we are confused, we can rely on these girlfriends to point the way to clarity and maybe even to give us the necessary boot to get started.

In May 1998, my husband and I decided to divorce. I had to somehow pull myself together and start my life over again. But the question was, "How?"

JoAnn, Adele, Sara, and Jenny knew that I was falling apart, but they never gave up on me. They encouraged me to go out and talk about everything that was bothering me. I can still remember the night I finally broke down and cried for hours. They each held me and told me that all they could do for me was be there for me, but only I could change myself. They told me, "No one can make you happy or love you unless you love yourself and make yourself happy."

Well, here I am one year later, May 1999. I am finally divorced, I have lost eighty pounds, gained back my self-esteem, and can finally look in the mirror and say, "I am Leyla and I am pretty, smart, happy, stronger, and I have four best friends that tell me every day how proud they truly are of me." —Leyla

I cared about Mandy so much that once I called her parents in a rage and told them they were too hard on her. I think she and her parents thought I was nuts, but after that they all definitely knew how much I cared about my friend. —*Jane*

A true girlfriend cares enough to get her hands dirty, even when she isn't asked for help. We might want our friends to leave us to our old ways, but these are the friends we need most when we get stuck.

Friends worth keeping stand up for us, stand up to us, and stand in for us in situations when we genuinely need to rely on their love.

A true friend keeps her mouth shut
when you start dating a loser but speaks up
when it gets too serious. —*Caroline*

Accepting the
Whole Package

*B*y feeling accepted, we learn to like ourselves more. When we like ourselves more, we can accept others and be more patient of what we think of as their foibles. By being more accepting of our friends, we may bring some balance into our own lives. The cycle that friendship provides is a worthwhile one to begin.

She's artistic and bold and sloppy and she went through this phase where she would not wear underwear, no matter what. She is loud, she belches in public, and she wears glitter on her face whenever she can. She is not ladylike. She is intensely loyal, rude, and speaks before thinking, so we know that she always tells the truth. She is also highly gullible and trusting. She's outgoing in the extreme, and the only predictable thing about her is that nobody ever knows what she's going to do next. We smack her around a lot. *–Colleen*

My inner circle of "soul friends," are women who don't shy away when I am angry, avoid me when I am sad or take it personally when I need to "blow off steam." *—Polly*

The best thing about girlfriends is that we can be whoever we are with them, and they will accept us anyway. It really does not matter to our close friends what we look like or what mood we're in.

Jill is married now. This is amazing to me because she is the biggest waffler I have ever known. I once sent her into a store to buy chips, and she was in there for thirty minutes trying to decide what kind to get. I had to go in there and fetch her and the chips or we would be there still. *—Colleen*

> She is my best friend even though she is terribly bossy. —*Elaine*

No one knows why feeling accepted, completely, faults and all, is so powerfully healing. We just know that we are transformed when someone else listens to us, taking in our experience.

She is a true girlfriend because she
keeps a straight face when others tell her
how sweet I am. —*Christine*

Sharing Our Burdens

*O*ne of life's most moving experiences is having a friend entrust us with the pain they feel. In fact, if we were excluded from caring for our girlfriends in times of need, we'd feel left out or cheated somehow.

When I moved to Connecticut, I reconnected with two friends I had known for years. We meet every month for lunch and a long visit (at least three or four hours) where we discuss everything from personal and marital dynamics to professional and intellectual topics. Sometimes we bring small gifts. Sometimes we bring copies of articles that we want to read and discuss together. I feel like a pregnant elephant, held up by the supportive bodies of the two females next to me. —*Suzy*

One morning a girlfriend of mine called just to check in. When one of my children answered and said, "Mommy's sick," she immediately got into her car and picked up and kept my three small children for the day. I was too sick to even argue, and she knew it.
—*Elizabeth*

A true girlfriend loans out her boyfriend to install your garbage disposal or fix your computer.
—*Karen*

In March, one of our group got cancer and it was we, her girlfriends, along with her kids, who took her to chemotherapy treatments, doctor visits, etc. We took her, swollen and hairless, on weekend jaunts to the seashore to get her out of her lonely apartment. At her funeral in October, we remaining seven sat and cried, but we understood her early death because Mary always had to be the first one to try everything. —*Sheila*

Who has not telephoned a friend and heard her say, "I am so relieved you called!"?

A true girlfriend will come to your house and do the task you hate to do most, like clean dog hair out from under the refrigerator. —*Glenda*

Dinah Shore wisely said, "Trouble is a part of your life, and if you don't share it, you don't give the person who loves you enough chance to love you enough."

I had to have intravenous treatments of corticosteroids for multiple sclerosis this year. Who showed up at 7:30 A.M. on a Sunday morning to sit with me while I had my treatment? My best friend. Who was there to listen when I was told I had precancerous cells and had to have a hysterectomy? My best friend. Who came to the hospital when I had my hysterectomy? My best friend. Who was there the same day she returned from her vacation when I had to have another treatment? My best friend— who else? —*Elizabeth*

I have many good friends, but this friendship is different. No one truly knows my pain from miscarrying twins except for my husband, and because Alexandra experienced a similar loss, it is so easy to share with her. Some weeks we focus heavily on our feelings about the miscarriage, and other weeks we talk about how far we've both come since that time. —*Mary Beth*

For sixteen years, four of my best women friends and I have met for each others' birthdays. For me, this has become one place where I can touch base with the past and be able to integrate the present. As time goes on, the ritual becomes more and more important, not because we need to celebrate another birthday, but because we need to sit with each other and laugh and cry about the latest events in each others' lives. We've chronicled births, deaths, sicknesses, weddings, and tears of joy and sadness. Three of us have divorced, two are widowed (one widowed twice), two have had cancer, one has had a miscarriage, and one has lost a child. Two were married, two children were born, and seven grandchildren were born. Through our shared book the message is clear, we all value having each other to share our joys and burdens with.

—*Lois*

We feel honored to share the weight of a girlfriend's grief.

I remember when my great grandma died. My friend skipped her play rehearsal to listen to me and cry with me and hand me tissues. That was the best thing anyone could've done. *—Jenee*

The burden of loss that is shared is lightened by the sharing of it, yet the one who picks up part of the load is not burdened in the same measure.

Since the death of my husband at age forty-two, twenty-two years ago, my sister-in-law has been a rock for me, especially when I was diagnosed with breast cancer. She flew cross country to take me out to buy a wonderful hat and to a photography studio to have our pictures taken, so that when I lost my hair, I could look at the photograph and look forward to growing it all back. —*Lois*

I've considered Tracy my very best friend ever since the day my husband was badly burned in an accident and required a six-week stay in the burn unit. Without a second thought, Tracy was at my door with suitcase in hand. She moved in with me and helped me with my not-quite-one-year-old son. Best of all, she let me cry when I was scared and didn't know what had happened to my storybook life. I am happy to say that it has been eighteen years since that awful day. That little baby is now in college, and I am still happily married.

—*Marsha*

She always knows exactly what I need to boost my spirits and is forever doing the things that bring huge smiles to my face. —*Aimee*

A true girlfriend shows up when your parents visit. —*Jean*

Throughout the three-and-a-half months my daughter was in a coma, and for the next year, Carol called me every day, sometimes twice a day, letting me know that she was there for me to talk to and to cry with. She gave me words of encouragement, sometimes calling just to say, "Hello, I was thinking about you today, and I love you."
—*Brenda*

My friend, a lawyer, did more than I could ever have expected in helping my family through a legal problem. She saved us. —*Melinda*

Most of us suffer losses and disappointments that seem insurmountable, but when we do not have the strength within ourselves, our girlfriends can loan us their hope, their passion, and their commitment to life so that, on borrowed faith, we can take the next step.

True girlfriends keep us sane, jump in
when necessary, and provide the silver lining
to a dark cloud (or at least a messy one).

Who Would I Be Without Her?

Shaping Each Other into Fabulous Women

*W*hether a friend travels with us for a short leg of the journey, for years, or for a lifetime, our bonds to other women serve as a source of comfort, wisdom, and direction, and shape the women we become.

My friends have given me life. They have helped me create myself. *—Catherine*

In the last note she wrote me before she left she said, "I truly believe that your friends make you who you are and I wouldn't be who I am today if it weren't for all those yesterdays with you." *—April*

Our close friends in varying degrees are women we trust, admire, respect, enjoy—with a strong dose of laughter, honesty, acceptance, and patience. In seeing ourselves in other feminine energy, we validate our journey and see that we have all the building blocks in force. *—Irene*

We discover ourselves through our girlfriends; it's a mutual process of self-discovery that goes on when we enter into this kind of female relationship. *—Sue*

Relating to my women friends makes me feel more intensely woman — not merely female but womanly. So much comfort, so sane. *—Marilyn*

Our friends affect our personalities, our appearances, and how we feel about ourselves in general. We look to our girlfriends to help us make sense of ourselves as women, which in this society often translates into how we look. We discuss our weight, dieting, exercise, clothes sizes, and our feelings about being too much or too little.

Friendship becomes stronger the more rites of passage we survive together — experiences so common in the lives of girls and women that they mark our shared growth. The more memories and transitions we share with our friends, the deeper and more complex the relationship.

She is still the person I most want to be like. —Gayle

Rene is the first person who taught me that it was acceptable to say "no," even to her. —Wendy

For as long as I can remember, I've tried to imitate the best attributes of my friends and make them part of my own personality. —Kathy

As do many women going through divorce, we both lost a lot of weight. Eileen is the one who decided I needed a new hairdo to go with my new body. She gave me so much more than a new hairstyle, she gave me a new image of myself and the base of a loving friendship. She helped me gain back my self-confidence. —*Sandra*

At the age of forty-nine, I decided to follow a dream of performance music, a dream I'd had all my life. I couldn't have made it without the encouragement of my friends. An unexpected gift was that my girlfriends saw my success and that inspired several of them to go after their potential. It's a thrill to see them so happy and fulfilled. —*Linda*

We look to women and their experiences in order to define ourselves as women, to value ourselves as women, to value ourselves as human beings.

Seeing ourselves differently, from the vantage points of our friends, can be so powerful at times, it can literally alter our perspective on life. Perhaps most profound is the realization that we are not alone.

True friends help us grow, even when we'd prefer to stay right where we are.

We Keep Each Other's Secrets

*C*ontrary to the myths of popular culture whereby women are supposedly unable to keep a secret, we found that confidentiality is an attribute most appreciated and respected by women.

Frequently a woman lets another woman know that she is her most trusted friend by sharing an aspect of herself that she has kept secret from the rest of the world.

I can express my dreams, fantasies, or fears without anxiety because I know they will remain in confidence and I won't be considered crazy. I can pick up the phone and call my friend Eleanor, even if it's just to say, "I just needed to say this out loud to someone." I know she will listen with love and acceptance, giving me her perspective if I ask for it or just lending a listening ear. —*Rene*

I trust her with my home, my money, and my boyfriend. Most importantly, however, I trust her with my secrets. —*Lisa*

I can tell Jasmine anything. Not only do I know that whatever secret I tell her is going to be kept confidential, but I can tell her things about myself or my actions that I am embarrassed to tell anyone else. She never makes me feel bad about myself, no matter what I tell her. It is not like she pooh-poohs my problems either. She always listens, and she will tell me what she honestly thinks without making me feel ashamed. —*Eleanor*

When I'm talking about a difficult subject, it's just easier not to actually be there looking at her. I can't really see her reaction, so I can just tell my story without being inhibited. I'm much more relaxed and able to talk openly when I'm on the phone. —*Molly*

Friends often provide a listening ear over the phone. Something about the telephone allows us to fully unburden ourselves. It is the modern confessional, the dark booth in which we are alone and yet not alone, where we can spill out the things about which we are most ashamed. By not having to face a friend, we can get the dark secrets or unexplainable feelings out.

Trustworthiness is about having faith that someone will keep your secrets, will react in a loving way to whatever you reveal, and accept you without making you feel ashamed.

Over the years I've known women who've proven to be impeccable human beings. Each one has taught me that trust is possible. *—Vicky*

Imagine the future. Our friends will be carrying with them all we've shared with them — our secrets, our dreams, our best and worst moments.

> We have entrusted our deepest, darkest moments to each other. A deep friendship allows for dependence upon each other as well as support, courage, and honesty. —*Tanya*

If you find a woman who can be trusted and who is willing to trust — keep her (along with the secrets she will entrust to you), and together you will build a bond that can withstand the test of time.

Where others may pass on bits of information as gossip, a true girlfriend values our confidences, protecting our private truths as she would her own, and accepts what we have to say without judgment.

She Tells Me True

Every woman needs a truth teller, and every relationship, in order to survive, requires that truth be told.

A friend is someone who is there for you in the good times and the bad and will be honest and truthful even if it hurts. They don't just tell you what you want to hear, they tell you the truth.
—Marsha

Our friends can help us view ourselves more positively because they are an honest mirror to see ourselves more accurately. The women who love us with a lifelong commitment have the boldness to tell it like it is.

Pat had been married for a number of years when I met my future husband. One week after we started dating, I took him to meet Pat and her husband because I knew she'd tell him how wonderful I was, right? Pat came in from the kitchen (looking like Donna Reed) and, wiping flour from her hands onto her apron, took his arm and immediately blurted out all of my most embarrassing moments: "Come into the kitchen with me while I tell you about Helen. Did you know she gets corn up her nose when she eats it on the cob? Did she ever tell you abut the time she peed in the elevator?" Now that's honesty for you! *—Helen*

Deciding when to push a friend and when to hold back can be complicated, and all a woman can do is use her unique knowledge of her friend to make the decision.

A girlfriend can sometimes see your situation more clearly than you can.

The quality I love most about her is when she is upset with me, or anything, she comes right up to me and says it. Sometimes I believe she could conquer the world. —*Lauren*

The relationship in which truth is told is one that can be trusted, and relationships that go through troubled times are strengthened by the test.

When you tell your girlfriends something that's bogus, you can hear it in your own ears as it comes out of your mouth. You know they know that they're keeping you honest about who you are, the way visiting home again keeps you honest about who you were. —*Stephanie*

At times it's important to be honest and say, "This is as far as I can go. I've reached my limit."

A girlfriend is one who can admit if she is upset with you and you can admit the same to her. Many of us raised as "good girls" fear conflict in a relationship because we do not realize that a real friendship can sustain the strain.

Friendship is limited when we are not honest with our friends, but also when we don't allow a friend to tell us what she perceives as the truth. We may not ultimately agree, but if a friend is trying to convey something, it's wise to take some time and listen.

A true girlfriend can tell you if your hair color is bad or if your boyfriend lied to you. The interesting thing is, so can your worst enemy. The difference is that your girlfriend does not relish it, and you somehow know that in your bones.

She Makes Me Bolder

I n spite of the stereotype that little girls are made of "sugar and spice and everything nice," we women know that we made quite a bit of mischief when we were younger. Of course, some of us continue that tradition and cause trouble when we are older—a good kind of trouble that comes from making up our own minds about life's rules, accepting the consequences of our actions, and, when needed, defending ourselves.

Individually we might have been ordinary women, but together we became Bette Midler thumbing our noses at prudence. —*Sue*

I remember the first time I met my angel, Jackie. I was terribly shy that first day but all that changed real quick. —*Jenee*

We misbehave so similarly, although in all other things we are very different. I still am more finicky, and she is more casual. Physically, she is dark-complected, about ten inches taller than I am, and always looking for extra-long pants; I am very fair-skinned with blond hair, and I shop in the children's department for my clothes. As we were cutting up in this class together, a woman turned to us and said, "Are you two twins?" We just looked at each other and laughed, but she was serious. I guess we are soul mates in making trouble.

—Glori

Whether it is poking fun at someone (who desperately deserves it) in order to maintain a sense of humor in a difficult situation, marching to stand up for a cause in which we believe, or sidestepping some regulations to accomplish a necessary objective, women need to stir up matters.

Often the fun that we enjoy with our girlfriends stems from letting the bad girls within out for a time. What is it about our friends' presence that inspires us to make mischief, take revenge, or strut our stuff? We not only laugh more, but we tend to laugh a little louder, and our plans get a tad more outrageous.

We share our vulnerabilities with each other and come away stronger. —*Lois*

Because of the support of the women in the class, her self-esteem had risen so much she could finally imagine someone loving her. She married soon after and I got to go to the wedding. —*Vicky*

It is so much fun for me to see my friends love what they are doing. I was very surprised when each woman told me I was her inspiration. —*Linda*

Women gain strength in groups; packs of women can get more accomplished than one woman alone. And working in a group can give us the courage and momentum to step in where we wouldn't necessarily have done so alone.

All we may need is a friend to share her strength, and we can become clear-headed and courageous again.

A little bit of nudging can go a long way. The encouragement we provide a friend often cycles back to inspire us as we see her accomplishing her goals.

The most challenging and certainly the most frightening adventure we can embark upon is one that brings risk into our lives. Many people dream of making changes or going after goals that seem beyond their grasp, but few have the courage, confidence, or self-esteem to single-handedly make the dream flesh-and-blood. Girlfriends can give us the extra push we need to go to those strange territories, to say "no" when we want to, to say "yes" when we want to (both without guilt), to set our boundaries, and to just generally live in a way more beneficial to ourselves.

A true girlfriend gives a push in the
right direction.

We Help Each Other Succeed

*I*t takes great courage to face both success and loss. Our girlfriends are those who stand with us proudly after we have made a tough decision or realized a longheld dream.

I'd always thought my true friends were revealed by what happens when times are tough, but recent experience proved that your true friends are those who can share the times that are really good for you. —*Laura*

Tracy and I have been best friends for twenty-seven years, and I think the secret to our friendship is our mutual respect for each other. Although our lives are so very different, we've always been so proud of each other's accomplishments. She is a very well-respected lawyer and happily married without children, and I am a happily married mother of two wonderful sons. I just went back to work last year, and our friendship grows stronger over the passing years. —*Marsha*

Success, too, is a transition, and a woman experiencing it may need her friends as much or more than when she seems beset with problems. What is success if we can't share it with our girlfriends?

When we spoke with Betty and Sara, they described coaching each other in their respective marital relationships. Betty talks about the effects of that coaching: "I probably will get to stay married to this man for the rest of my life. A few years ago, when Jeff and I weren't having such a good time, Sara said, 'You're not leaving him. I'll nail your shoes to the floor.'"

Sara interrupted to remind her gently, "No, it was your feet I threatened to nail to the floor. You can walk out of your shoes."

Betty, remembering, nodded in agreement. "I think about that image all the time. We want each other's relationships to work."

❦

When we take that daring trip, put our hand out to receive that diploma, or walk into an office for an interview for that coveted job, we know that our girlfriends share in the sweet taste of victory.

My friends didn't want me to poison my marital relationship with anger, which left me the option of reconstructing my relationship with my husband. Now our relationship is much better than it ever was, partly because my friends taught me how to be loyal to myself and how to focus my energies on taking care of me instead of being angry with my husband. —*Natasha*

How many of us would be where we are today, with the accomplishments we have obtained, without our girlfriends telling us, "I know you can do it!"?

A true girlfriend holds your purse
while you dance with the only cute guy
in the place. —*Laura*

Bumps Along
the Way

When a Friendship Is in Trouble

*T*he bond between women can be challenged when changes that come with growing up and growing old confront a friendship.

> You know when you have your answering machine turned on because you're afraid your friend is going to call, something is wrong with the friendship. —*Kathleen*

If boundaries can never be respected by one of us, or if one of us is always the needy one and never able to offer help to the other, the relationship is not a healthy one for either of the friends.

I think when you chronically misperceive someone or they chronically misperceive you, that's usually something that you almost can't get around. —*Michiko*

If we cannot respect the decisions our friends are making, or we cannot adapt to the changes they choose to make, the friendship will ultimately not last.

> Perhaps one of the most painful moments in a friendship is when one girlfriend realizes that her friend needs or wants more than she can give.

Helen was a snob. I realized that early on, but I ignored it because she never treated me unequally. Until the day she told me that my husband was too physically attractive for me, that I had a man whom someone much prettier than me deserved. It has been a year since we have conversed. It hurts to have lost a "friend for life." —*Ronnie*

When trust is missing, friendships stand little chance of deepening and may instead fade away in the future.

One sure way to lose a friend is to pretend you are not hurt when you actually are, or to try to hide your anger.

Problems arise for those who do not make room for their girlfriends' partners, often forcing their girlfriends to choose between them and their romantic lovers. When an ultimatum is given, the romantic partner is usually chosen and the girlfriend is left behind.

Our friends are so important to us that when one of them deserts us, we miss her terribly. Not only does the betrayal hurt, but we have lost the person to whom we would normally have gone for comfort.

A true friendship is in trouble when you pick and choose what you reveal.

Getting Through the Rough Parts

*R*ocky periods in friendships tend to be like broken bones—painful and debilitating but, once healed, making the relationship stronger than ever.

Disagreements have been part of our relationship—along with forgiveness—as we are totally different personalities and love always remains.
—*Claudette*

I felt that I was in crisis, and I needed her to be calling, but it's true that I didn't let her know exactly what I needed. I felt abandoned because she didn't initiate toward me, and she felt that I needed to be more clear about what I needed from her. It's clear that we both have areas to work on in this relationship. —*Sabrina*

Part of being a good friend and having good friends is being willing to stay in there and fight.

> Making the leap—allowing yourself to be vulnerable and speak out when you notice something feels wrong in the friendship—requires courage and commitment.

We stopped talking to each other for almost two years because of something that really did seem important at the time. I said that she and I would never be friends the way we had been, but all she had to do in the end was reach out to me and there I was. —*Colleen*

It may take years to approach each other, but it is never too late to try to clear up a sore spot in a relationship.

Eventually I went over to my friend's house with a twelve-pack of beer. When she opened the door, I said, "You know, we really need to talk." She immediately broke down. We talked about it, and it felt so good to have it out right there. A year and a half later I was maid of honor at her wedding. We're still close. —*Dana*

Commitment to each other is the foundation to longevity, a commitment which includes the gumption to face conflict and wrestle to resolution.

A friendship that becomes lopsided can be a relationship winding down. Both women need to be able to ask for what they need and place limits on what they give. This delicate balance is rarely, if ever, maintained perfectly, so hurt feelings, misunderstandings, and forgiveness are required for the bond to endure.

During our junior year in high school, my best friend and I had an argument that split us up for more than a year. By the end of our senior year, I had decided that our differences weren't enough to keep me from seeing her graduate. I found her after the ceremony, expecting to be told I had no right to be there. Instead, we took one look and fell into each other's arms. We picked right up where we left off. The events that parted us were forgiven and forgotten. I couldn't tell you what that fight was about now if my life depended upon it. —*Tracey*

Apologies and forgiveness combine to make the magic that gets us beyond mistakes and helps us set our relationships right.

A true girlfriend shows up with chocolate after a fight and is still willing to share.

When We Go in Opposite Directions

*T*he freedom shared by lifelong friends lets women follow their sometimes very different paths and yet continue to celebrate their friendship throughout their lives.

When her dad got transferred and she had to move to Georgia I was crushed. I felt like I was losing my right arm or my other half.
—Jenee

She went to college on the East Coast, while I went to Colorado. As soon as I got there, I missed her so much that I used my book money to buy an airplane ticket and flew to Vermont to surprise her. I just got on a plane and landed in Middlebury and wandered around until I found the college. We have lived very different lives, and yet we will always be good friends. She will always be a part of my life. *—Nancy*

I remember our last day of college vividly. We were moving our remaining belongings out of our rooms (only across the hall from each other). Suddenly I looked over at her and realized that we would never live this close to each other again. I felt sick. How could I live (or spell) without her? I quickly shoved the rest of my stuff in a bag, wiped away a tear, and acted like I was just going down for another trip to my car. But it was the last trip. I couldn't say good-bye to her—partly because I would instantly begin weeping and partly because I knew this wasn't really good-bye. —*Jane*

If friends can make room for each other when they are making changes in their lives, they can set the groundwork for sharing a great number of life experiences that will come their way, each at different times and with varying impact.

After college we lost touch for years. On the death of her brother, we got back together and spent a weekend at her home in Galveston. After food, fun, and laughs, we each admitted to the other that we were really afraid that we would no longer have anything in common. In fact, it was as if time had stood still. *—Rhonda*

Our bond defies time. Our paths may not cross for the longest time, but when we get back together it's as if no time has passed. *—Arlene*

One of the true tests of friendship is asking for support and encouragement from a girlfriend in making a decision that results in leaving that girlfriend behind.

We have to remember not to take our friend's choices personally—she is probably not getting married, moving to take a new job, or having a baby because she is trying to avoid us! If a friend's life changes, we should graciously respect and adjust to this change.

Only those who really love you can encourage you to follow your dream or take a step that is good for you, even it means they will not be with you as much as they perhaps would like. This kind of support can further strengthen an already strong bond and is a good sign that a friendship will last.

Marriage and babies do not need to mark the end of a relationship, even though it may indeed signify the end of an era in that relationship. Recognizing that no one can take your place in your girlfriend's life is a necessary aspect of maintaining a relationship that can span a lifetime.

If we are the ones doing the changing, a simple declaration of devotion to our friend ("My life is taking a different turn, but I need you more then ever because of it!") can go a long way toward assuaging her fear that you might be dropping out of her life forever.

Whether the cord of independence stretches to allow for emotional space or spans years of separation, it is strong and unbreakable, eventually drawing us back to one another. And when we return to share the stories of our adventures, we have the opportunity to celebrate our differences and take pride in our loose-fitting, but lasting bonds.

I know she is my best friend because she lets me use her storage space, even when I am moving away from her. —*Amanda*

Enjoying Our Differences (and Accepting Our Faults)

*A*s we mature, we may find ourselves drawn to women we perceive as different from ourselves—women who would have intimidated us or made us uncomfortable in previous times of our lives. This attraction may be a signal that we are developing a new aspect of ourselves.

We may choose a friend because we admire her, and yet, in admiration, aren't we expressing who and what we would like to become? Perhaps we are ripe for some new growth, and our friend will facilitate that development.

On the surface, I don't think anyone would think my best friend and I would be attracted to each other—she is shy and somewhat introverted, and I am more aggressive and outgoing. But somehow we recognized each other at a level that I don't believe was conscious. We knew right away we would be good, good friends. Today, five years later, she is one of the most important people in my life.

—Jeanne

We describe our friendship as "looking in a mirror." We are so much alike and yet different. We agree on most things and when we disagree we always find a happy medium. We have seen each other through deaths, boyfriends, fights with parents, everything! *—Julia*

I think of two of my closest friends, Christi and Jill, like this: They are really a lot alike, but Jill is the Prozac version of Christi—like the before and after pictures. Christi is before electroshock therapy, and Jill is after. —*Colleen*

She and her husband have three children and live a very simple Mennonite lifestyle committed to world peace and the environment. On the other hand, in college I was pro-Vietnam, voted Republican, and continue to be her opposite. I've always lived in large cities, have traveled internationally, and have two graduate degrees. And yet, once a year we come together, and we'll spend about thirty-six hours together. We stay up the whole night, talking and enjoying our rituals. I always bring a jar of Ovaltine, and we make popcorn and talk all night long. —*Robin*

Commonalities? Differences? What brings us together and makes a relationship work? Maybe in some cases we find someone who, rather than insisting on being like us, is simply willing to like us—differences, similarities, warts, and all.

She is a true friend because she ignores
the sucking sound at the end of the phone when
I am "sneaking" a cigarette. —*Pamela*

Tributes, Praise, and Memories

Friendships with a Future

*H*aving a friend for life does not require that we know each other from childhood (although some do), that we be the same age (although many friends are), that we share similar traits (although many friends will), or even that we like each other at first (although many are immediately drawn to each other).

No matter where we are in our life's journey, we all have a future to imagine. Often we can tell who our best girlfriends are by whether we see them in our future plans.

Today, as we mark twenty years of friendship, I am grateful to my brother for bringing Laurie into my life. Grateful for a friend who knows without being told, does without asking, gives without taking. Someone who understands when the whole world doesn't. And I'm joyous in anticipation of what the next twenty years have in store for us.

—Judy

Friendships that are honored by a symbol, or a regularly scheduled celebration are more likely to survive than those in which long periods of time pass without acknowledgment. Once we indicate how important a girlfriend is to us, we strengthen the bond and invigorate the relationship itself.

As women look to the future and growing old together, many express a vision with a sense of security and joyful anticipation. In the past, a woman planning her senior years may have looked solely to family members. Today's women, however, often include girlfriends in those plans as well.

> Friends worth keeping forever often surprise us with their devotion, their laughter, and their affection.

> The bond that we forged so many years ago is now unbreakable. —*Gayle*

Our friendship has gone through what I would call "phases." We've seen each other through the establishment of lives separate from our families, seen jobs and careers evolve, relationships come and go, but the one constant seems to be our friendship. The characteristic that has enabled us to make it through these phases has been a commitment to communication. We have always made it a priority to keep in contact with each other. Sometimes it has not been easy, for schedules, jobs, and other relationships can be so seductive — can dominate our attention. I suppose there are to be many more phases to our friendship, but I am convinced that our trust in and commitment to each other will enable us to make the necessary adjustments. —*Rene*

No one can predict the future, but our determination to stay connected to each other, whether it is for the next year or the next fifty, gives us a vision for the future and joy for today.

A friend for life knows us well, and with that knowledge, is cued into how we may be affected by the events of daily life. Her knowledge, and the use of it, expresses how she cares about us and our relationship.

In March of 1994, I was rushed to the hospital and told I had a rare neurological disorder. When I returned to work, I got a phone call from a co-worker. She herself was just diagnosed with breast cancer and was pregnant, and she took the time to call me to see if I needed anything. I *never* forgot that. —*Elizabeth*

> Beth is Wednesday Addams in the body of the girl-next-door. She is beautiful, fearless, dramatic, and weird. The more time I spend with Beth, the more layers I uncover. I wonder if I'll ever figure her out all the way, then again, I don't want to. I sort of feel that if I were to dig at her with my analytical brain, some of her magic would be stolen. Beth is meant to be an enigma. —*Colleen*

Every healthy, loving relationship between two people requires that both individuals be able to tolerate the differences between them. Friends for life may share many things, but still have differing tastes in everything from what they eat to the life partners they choose. Respect for those choices and support of the differences can enrich the friendship and the friends' lives, as they witness, and participate in, each other's life paths.

Perhaps one of the most important qualities of a long-term friendship is the ability to allow room for growth and change.

The more we let our girlfriends know how much they are valued, the stronger our friendships grow.

A true friend knows never to ask me to host or even attend a Tupperware, make-up, or basket home party. *—Elizabeth*

Friendships may shift and alter, they may strengthen and weaken, but the bond of a true girlfriend can never, ever be broken. *—Allison*

I Love Her . . .

I love her even though she's perfect and her
linen never wrinkles.

I love her because she thinks every man is
flirting with me.

I love her even though she ignores my advice—
she asks, I give, she ignores. —*Becky*

I love her even though she always orders
the most fattening thing on the menu, eats it,
then finishes off my dinner, and weighs
half what I do. —*Janet*

Memories for a Lifetime

*T*he creation of traditions, rituals, and symbols shows that we have made a permanent place for our friends in our lives and acknowledges the contribution those friends make to the quality of our experience. Traditions and rituals ground us, letting us know that we are still there for each other.

Maggie and I have a very meaningful tradition: We have sent the same plastic poinsettia back and forth with our Christmas gifts each year for the last twenty years. —*Kathleen*

Carey plans a river rafting trip every year for her women friends, which she calls "Amazons Down the River."

We keep journals of our times together and let each other read them. How much fun it is to share what the other has remembered. —*Jean*

What their friendship has given me is a diary of my life. Because I keep copies of my letters to them, I have a diary going back fifteen years or more. I keep their notes and letters and someday plan to send them back to them so they may remember those bits and pieces of life often forgotten unless written down. —*Theresa*

Friends hold our memories for us and reflect back to us things about ourselves and our lives that we had buried in some inaccessible place in our minds.

Our senior year in high school, Karen and I exchanged yearbooks. I remember looking at her picture and I couldn't think of anything to write. Here we were, best friends, emotional intimates. We'd been in class together, had even gotten caught by the teacher for duplicating each other's homework assignment, and no words would come. I looked at Karen and she at me. Simultaneously and silently we handed the books back to each other. It seemed more fitting to let them stay clean, unsigned, untied to that particular era of our lives. The open space itself symbolized our feelings about each other—that we would be in touch forever, in a constant change that wouldn't be confined to the words below a peterpan-collar photograph. *—Suzy*

Our memories are so abundant and rich; our influence on each other has been profound. We have argued with teachers on each other's behalf, forged parents' signatures in the name of friendship, told each other's ex-boyfriends what louses they were, held hands walking through unfamiliar hallways together, and we still laugh at the part in the movie no one else finds funny. —*Tanya*

We sat on a Hawaiian beach and she taught me how to spit watermelon seeds. —*Rena*

Showing appreciation is an important component of friendships that last.

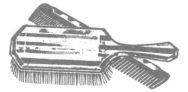

One birthday, I sent Karen fourteen numbered postcards, each with one letter on it; together they spelled out HAPPY BIRTHDAY. (I even sent a blank card for the space between the words.) Despite being sent out one at a time, they arrived over a space of three days. Karen was puzzled at first and then enjoyed the thought and joke as the postcards arrived. —*Suzy*

My cousin Ann Frances and I have been close girlfriends since we were born, I guess. We're a year apart and our mothers dressed us alike. She was good at hair, make-up, and clothes and practiced on me. I accompanied on the piano as we sang one Broadway musical after another. During one particular Thanksgiving family gathering, "the cousins" balked at the traditional religious service we normally performed, and Ann Frances and I instead performed a few musical selections dressed as Richard and Karen Carpenter. She, being the brunette, was Karen. I, the blond piano player, had no choice but to be Richard. —*Elizabeth*

A shared cup of tea every Tuesday morning after the kids are off to school, a few minutes together in each other's offices over a soda, pasta and movies every Thursday night, a hike or a poetry reading once a month, even an annual reunion especially planned to review the previous year of your lives and plan the future: These are remembered traditions that honor a friendship.

There are these huge thunderstorms, and we sit out on the porch in rocking chairs with coffee and talk, and comes the dawn. *—Robin*

Of course you can go home again! You just look in your heart for your old best friend! *—Helen*

Because our friendships help shape us in myriad ways, we take our girlfriends with us long after we can no longer hear their voices or see their smiles.

One day at work, a particularly trying day, Becki dropped by, unannounced, to say hi and also to bring me a gift: a small decorative can filled with candy. I can't tell you how that small gesture helped me get through the day. It was a note of cheer that I will always remember. When the can was empty, instead of pushing it in the corner of a closet or tossing it, I decided to fill it with something small and return it—hence the launching of the Friendship Can and a deeper level to our friendship. —*Dode*

We remember things when the other one has forgotten them, and then it's like giving each other something back. —*Arlene*

The ritual of the five of us meeting regularly has become one constant in a life of inconstants, one place where I can touch base with the past and be able to integrate the present. —*Lois*

We have spent New Year's Eve together for about thirty years, sometimes with many other people, sometimes with just a few. It is something we never, ever want to give up. —*Jane*

I was with her constantly during her last two weeks before breast cancer got the best of her. I lost her a little over a year ago and have just recently been able to make it through a full day without an almost physical ache of sorrow when thinking of her. It may be slow but, at some point, memories of your best friend bring comfort, not just sorrow. —*Peggy*

> We are each other's life historians. *—Jackie*

Our get-togethers that started with simple cookies and coffee have developed into lavish meals and a yearly, full-day progressive meal for Christmas. Now that our children are growing up, we have more opportunities to spend time together. We are looking forward to going out for lunches, shopping trips, and visiting other places. We know that whatever the future holds, we will be there for each other. *—Cheri*

A friendship varied in its history, peppered with conflict as well as accord, is one that becomes more and more valuable. As we go through difficult times as well as enjoyable ones, we create rich layers of experience that test and ultimately strengthen the friendship. What results is a lush tapestry of memories shared with your friend.

My thirtieth birthday was on March twenty-ninth and my roommate was leaving April first. I felt abandoned and lonely. On my birthday, I got a huge bouquet of tulips from Leslie, and the card said, "I'll always be here for you." I still have that card, which I look at all the time. It's really true. That was the beginning of our tradition of sending each other flowers on our birthdays, and that was the first card of many I've received from her. It was what I needed then, and every time I read the card, I know I still need it. *—Elise*

Our friendship is a running list of incredible memories. We have gone dancing to big band music in Disneyland as childhood buddies, we have gone to art shows and seen our own work displayed side by side. We have trekked throughout San Francisco on foot, finding the little paths and pockets of beauty often forgotten. We have watched the flock of green parrots that live next to her house squawk in the tree, and eaten raw tomatoes on rocks by the ocean. And we have declared ourselves spiritual sisters. We are wild women, dancing through our lives in grace and intensity, even more so with the help of our eclectic friendship. *—Vanessa*

A true friend stays.

Personal Quotes